ROUTLEDGE LIBRARY EDITIONS:
JAPAN

AN ESSAY ON THE CIVILISATIONS OF INDIA, CHINA & JAPAN

AN ESSAY ON THE CIVILISATIONS OF INDIA, CHINA & JAPAN

G. LOWES DICKINSON

Volume 32

Routledge
Taylor & Francis Group
LONDON AND NEW YORK

First published in 1914

This edition first published in 2011
by Routledge
2 Park Square, Milton Park, Abingdon, Oxon, OX14 4RN

Simultaneously published in the USA and Canada
by Routledge
711 Third Avenue, New York, NY 10017

Routledge is an imprint of the Taylor & Francis Group, an informa business

First issued in paperback 2013

British Library Cataloguing in Publication Data
A catalogue record for this book is available from the British Library

ISBN 13: 978-0-415-58533-0 (hbk)
ISBN 13: 978-0-415-84605-9 (pbk)

Publisher's Note
The publisher has gone to great lengths to ensure the quality of this reprint but points out that some imperfections in the original copies may be apparent.

Disclaimer
The publisher has made every e ffort to trace copyright holders and would welcome correspondence from those they have been unable to trace.

AN ESSAY ON THE
CIVILISATIONS of INDIA CHINA & JAPAN

G. LOWES DICKINSON

This Essay is a Report of the author's travels as a Fellow of the Albert Kahn Travelling Fellowships and is published by direction of the Albert Kahn Trustees.

TO THE TRUSTEES OF THE ALBERT KAHN TRAVELLING FELLOWSHIPS

GENTLEMEN,

I have the honour to present the following report of my travels during the years 1912 to 1913.

Instead of describing my journey in detail I have thought it will be more interesting to offer some reflections on the general spirit and character of the civilisations of India, China, and Japan, and the apparent and probable effects upon these civilisations of contact with the West. Any conclusions one may arrive at on a subject so comprehensive are, of course, of the most tentative and hazardous kind, and what I set down here is rather the starting point than the end of an inquiry. I shall not, however, waste time and space in constantly qualifying and apologising for my statements;

but say here, once for all, that everything put forward is provisional, and that any dogmatism of form is merely a concession to the requirements of brevity.

G. LOWES DICKINSON.

KING'S COLLEGE, CAMBRIDGE.
November 1913.

AN ESSAY ON THE CIVILISATIONS OF INDIA CHINA AND JAPAN

PART I.—INDIA

THE first thing I have to note is that the East is not a unity, as implied in the familiar antithesis of East and West. Between India, on the one hand, and China or Japan, on the other, there is as great a difference as between India and any western country. The contrast that has struck me is that between India and the rest of the world. There I do feel a profound gulf. A Chinese, after all, is not so unlike an Englishman, and a Japanese not so unlike a Frenchman. But a Bengalee is strangely unlike anybody outside India. While, however, the East is not a unity, the *modern* West is. Throughout Europe and America there is the same civilisation, intellectual and economic; so that, to a philosophic observer, national boundaries there already begin to appear obsolete and irrelevant. On the other hand, this modern West is a very recent creation. And if one goes back in history one can find more analogy between East and West than now appears. Feudal Europe, for example, was in many respects similar to feudal Japan; and a mediæval Christian mystic hardly distinguishable from a contemporary Indian saint. If, therefore, we contrast East and West we shall find our contrast breaking down at every point, unless we confine the term East to India (which is absurd), and mean by the West (as of course, in fact, we do) the West of the last century only. And the contrast between *that* West and the West of the Middle Ages is perhaps as great as the contrast between the modern West and India. I think it best, therefore, not to attempt to characterise the East as a whole; but to deal separately with India, China, and Japan, and their reactions to the West, as they have shown themselves to me. I shall endeavour to characterise each of these civilisations, first, as they were before contact with the West; and afterwards to consider the effect upon them of that contact.

To summarise, I will say, first, that I conceive the dominant note of India to be religion; of China, humanity; of Japan, chivalry. These terms, of course, to begin with, are mere labels. I shall proceed to develop my meaning in each case.

In discussing the religion of a people one is met with the perhaps insuperable difficulty of estimating what, to the mass of the people, their religious observances really mean. I think it is clear that to the peasants of most countries—of Italy, say, or of China or of Japan—religion is no more than a ritual which they would be uncomfortable if they did not perform; a kind of lightning conductor for the emotions and desires that are concerned with the ordinary business of life, with getting one's living, with birth, marriage, child-bearing, and death. And, of course, in India[1] religion is, at least, this. The people pray for children, pray for healing, pray for rain, pray for everything they want. But is not religion to Indians something more than this? Observers who try to know the people believe that it is, and I am inclined to think that they are

[1] In speaking of Indian religion I have in view throughout Hinduism, not Mahometanism.

right; that even the Indian peasant does really believe that the true life is a spiritual life; that he respects the saint more than any other man; and that he regards the material world as ' unreal," and all its cares as illusion. He cannot, of course, and does not, put this conviction into practice, or Indian society would come to an end. But he admires and even worships those who do put it into practice. I have seen on the faces of poor Indians, at religious functions, an expression I have seen nowhere else, unless, perhaps, in Russian churches. At Muttra, for instance, I remember the ecstatic look on the faces of the crowd as the priests waved their torches before the image of the god; and similarly, at Kandy, the look of those who came to worship the relics—books even!—at the Temple of the Tooth. This is "idolatry," of course. But what does idolatry imply? Roman Catholics choose to think that while Christians worship the god symbolised by the image, Chinese or Indians worship the image itself. But this is sheer prejudice. And, unless I am very much mistaken, an idol is far more of a symbol and less of an object of worship to an Indian peasant than it is to most Roman Catholics.

Kali is a hideous idol, fed by the blood of goats. But I am inclined to believe what I have been told, that to an Indian she symbolises the divine mother; and that it is her, not the idol, that they are worshipping.

I have said thus much on a very difficult subject, because I am taking the view that religion is the dominant factor in Indian society; and I wished to deal beforehand with the objection likely to be taken that very few Indians are religious in any true or important sense of the term. Very few, I agree, do or could carry through their religion to its logical consequences; but most have it; and most admire those who carry it out. This religion, however, is radically different from the religion of the Western nations. In the first place, India has never put Man in the centre of the universe. In India, and wherever Indian influence has penetrated, it is, on the one hand, the tremendous forces of nature, and what lies behind them, that is the object of worship and of speculation; and, on the other hand, Mind and Spirit; not the mind or spirit of the individual person, but the universal Mind, or Spirit, which is in him, but to which he can only have access by philosophic meditation and ascetic discipline. Indian religion is thus very "inhuman" compared to Christianity; and very much more in harmony with the spirit of western science than with that of western religion. And this fact is exemplified not only by the religious and philosophic literature of India, but by its art. Hindu sculpture and architecture—I have examined it from north to south, and from east to west—is disquieting and terrible to a western mind. It expresses the inexhaustible fertility, the ruthlessness, the irrationality of nature; never her beauty, her harmony, her adaptability to human needs. Man, in the Indian vision, is a plaything and slave of natural forces; only by ceasing to be man does he gain freedom and deliverance.

And this brings me to the second point in which Indian religion contrasts with that of the West. To an Indian saint or philosopher the whole world of matter is unreal, and the whole of human history illusory. There is no meaning in time or the processes of time; still less is there any goodness in it. In some way, unexplained and inexplicable, the terrible illusion we call life dominates mankind. To be delivered from the illusion—from life, that is, and activity in time—is the object of all effort and all religion. In this sense the Indian religion is pessimistic. There is, of course, an important distinction between Buddhism and the Brahminism it supplanted for a time and then succumbed to. Gautama Buddha, it would seem, was a thorough-going sceptic and rationalist; he believed neither in God nor in the soul; and the object of his teaching was to deliver men from life to annihilation by instructing them how to eliminate desire. Brahminism, on the other hand, wishes to deliver them from false life to true life. The true life is life eternal; and we may have access to it by discipline and meditation. But from my immediate point of view this distinction is not important. What is important is that, in either form, precisely that is denied which the West most emphatically affirms: the reality and importance of the material world, and of the historic process in time. The West is often called materialistic as compared with the East. But this antithesis, so far as it is true, does not depend on any metaphysical view held or denied as to the nature of matter. The West does not profess to know what matter is, and its hypotheses about it are always changing. The real point of distinction is, that the West believes that all effort ought to centre upon the process of living in time; that that process has reality and significance; and that the business of religion is not to deliver us from effort by convincing us of its futility, but to sanctify and justify it. No modern western man would regard as an admirable type at all—still less as the highest type—a man who withdraws from the world to meditate and come into direct contact with the Universal. But an Indian who is uncontaminated by western culture still regards that as the true ideal of conduct; and views all activities in the world as lower and inferior, though, for undeveloped men, they are necessary and pardonable.

With this view of religion the history and institutions of Hinduism harmonise. The Vedas, it is true, reflect an attitude to life similar to that of the Western Aryans; but this essentially active, positive, optimistic view gradually clouds over. The cause, perhaps, is the influence of climate, of a Nature too strong for man. No impression remains more vivid with me of my visit to India than that of the dominance of nature, and the impotence and insignificance of man. But whatever the cause, there is no doubt about the fact. Indian society became impregnated with the sense of the nothingness of life in time. To escape, not to dominate, became the note of their religion. And life being insignificant, history, of course, was so too. It is not an accident, it is a consequence of their attitude to life, that there are no Hindu historians. Contrast the Mahometans, contrast the Chinese, contrast the western nations. How can you write the history of a nightmare? You don't do that. You try to wake up.

It is true that Christianity, too, has, as one of its elements, this idea of the illusoriness of the world. But Christianity contains other elements, incompatible with this; as, indeed, it was its practical wisdom and its philosophic insufficiency that it combined the most irreconcilable notions. And further, the western nations have never really been Christian. Their true religion has only become apparent as Christianity has declined. That religion—not yet expressed in forms, but implicit in all their conduct—is that the time-process is also the real process; that everything material matters very much indeed; and that spiritualism must either recognise the claims of matter or retire from the conflict. This life and its purposes are significant, and important, and what a man ought to attend to; that is the real postulate of the modern West; and that is what all Indian religion and philosophy has denied. But on this point China and Japan are at one with the West. And that is why I said that the real antithesis is not between East and West, but between India and the rest of the world.

This, then, of general attitude towards life, carrying with it a whole psychology, and reflecting itself in religion and in art, is the first point that distinguishes the civilisation of India, as I think, from every other. The second point is one of social institutions. India is the home of caste. Caste may be defined as the hereditary determination of a man's place in society. No hard and fast line can be drawn between it and class; for wherever there are classes the position of the father plays some part, and usually the chief part, in determining the position of the son. Moreover, almost all societies—China is the great exception—have passed through an age of caste; Egypt, of course, *par excellence*, Japan, Europe in the

Middle Ages. But in India caste has developed into a rigour and a multiplicity unknown in any other country. Castes and sub-castes are innumerable, and new ones are always springing up. India has never been democratic, either in theory or in practice; never had the ideal of equal opportunity; always had that of hierarchy; and at the head of that hierarchy always the priest. Nothing, of course, could be more radically antagonistic to the whole current of theory and practice in the modern West. But this antagonism does not exist at all in the case of China, and only in a very modified degree in the case of Japan. Here, too, the position of India is unique. It is the antithetic pole to the West.

What I have said so far applies to India before contact with the West, and very generally and widely applies still. But a process of modification has been proceeding since the British conquest. And I will go on now to say what I have to say on this subject.

Here, again, India differs radically from China and Japan. China, though she has been bullied and robbed, has not been conquered and administered by the western powers. That may come. But, at any rate, up to now China has been an independent country. And Japan has not only saved her independence, she has energetically reacted against the West, and shown that she can give as well as take blows. But India, never a nation, never a unity, split up by racial, religious, caste distinctions, fell, and was bound to fall, an easy prey to a western power. That that power should be England is one of the ironies of history; for of all the western nations the English are the least capable of appreciating the qualities of Indian civilisation, and the most capable of appreciating its defects. To an Englishman, practical efficiency, honesty, and truth are the chief and indispensable goods. To an Indian, as, in a less degree, to other Orientals, all these things are indifferent. On the other hand, an Englishman has no conception even of the meaning of a philosophic or religious problem. The notion that the material world could be a mere illusion is one that could never appeal to him as even intelligible (Berkeley, it must be remembered, was an Irishman, and Hume a Scotchman). His religion, when he has one, is a transfigured morality, not a mysticism.

He is practical, through and through, in spiritual as well as in material things. Between him and the Indian the gulf is impassable.

Add to this that whereas all the other conquerors of India had migrated to the country, settled down and lived there, and become assimilated to Indian conditions, the English are, of all races, the least assimilable. They carried to India all their own habits and ways of life; squatted, as it were, in armed camps; spent as in exile twenty or twenty-five years; and returned home, sending out new men to take their place, equally imbued with English ideals and habits, equally unassimilable. Facility of communication has only emphasised and strengthened this attitude. The Englishman sends his children home to be educated; commonly his wife will spend at least half her time at home; he himself returns every few years; his centre is not India, but England. It would, I think, be unreasonable and absurd to blame the Englishman for this; he is, indeed, often praised for it by foreigners. As a very intelligent and enlightened official remarked to me, an Englishman cannot be expected to lose his own soul—and his soul is the traditions and habits of his race—for the sake of other people's politics. Still, there is the fact, and it is one of cardinal importance in the relations between the two races. It maintains the distinction between the governing and the governed people; and it does so by creating an almost impassable social gulf. For this gulf, however, it must in fairness be added, the Indians are not less responsible than the English. Their family and caste system hampers all social intercourse. If a man cannot eat with you, or introduce his wife to you, it is difficult for you to associate with him at all. Add to this that, whereas to most Englishmen sport and games are the main subjects, outside their work, of interest and conversation, to most Indians they are completely indifferent. Indians want to talk philosophy and religion; Englishmen want to talk polo and golf. There is no need, then, to suppose any kind of original sin or deliberate unkindness or wickedness on either side to account for the social chasm. Cases, it is true, still occur where individual Englishmen—generally, I think, in the army—are insolent to individual Indians, but these are becoming rarer, and are steadily discountenanced by

Government. They are not the root of the difficulty. The difficulty lies deeper; and I see no way of removing it, short of removing the English from India.

If the English had been able and content to govern Indians by the sword, without affecting their ideas and institutions, this social gulf need not perhaps have created a political difficulty. Indian civilisation would have proceeded unchanged, and Indians would have been indifferent as to who it was that raised the taxes, so long as they were not intolerably oppressive. But, in fact, it would have been impossible to govern India without modifying it; and in any case that was a policy deliberately rejected by the English. They determined to educate the Indians in English ideas; and they started this process at a moment peculiarly favourable to its success. For the old Indian education was in decadence, and Indians knew and cared little about their own philosophy. Under the new influences a generation grew up sceptical and rationalistic, nourished on Mill and Spencer, cut off from its own roots and artificially grafted on to the western tree. This, however, is only what happens and is bound to happen wherever

East meets West. The paradox in India is that the English have deliberately instructed their Indian subjects in their own political ideas; in a system of thought, therefore, which radically condemns the kind of government they maintain in India. Self-government, no taxation without representation, these and the like are the watchwords of English political philosophy; while English history supplies striking examples of the refusal of a people to submit to an arbitrary and autocratic government. In this philosophy and this history Indians are carefully educated. And further, they have before them the famous proclamation of 1858, that in the government of India no distinction shall be made on the ground of colour, race, or religion. It was genuinely believed by the statesmen who inaugurated this *régime* that under the new system of education the Indians would quickly become willing and able to administer their own country on English lines, under the aegis of English protection. And, in fact, as is well known, in the civil administration of India less than a thousand Englishmen take part; all subordinate posts are held by Indians; while in the judiciary the highest positions are open to natives of the country. Both in the central and provincial governments there are legislative and executive councils on a representative basis; and Lord Morley's recent reform has largely increased the power and prestige of these bodies. In the history of India, indeed, the critical point seems to have been reached at which any further extension of the principle of self-government would really transfer the control of the country from the English to the natives. And this, of course, would mean a real revolution, analogous to the change of water into steam or into ice when a certain point is reached in the heating or cooling process. Whether that next step shall be taken or not is the problem before which the government of India is hesitating.

There are two points here involved; first, the efficiency of a government controlled wholly or in part by Indians; secondly, its loyalty to the English political system.

When I was in India the Commission on the Indian Civil Service was sitting, and I had the opportunity of attending their meetings in Madras, and of talking with many of the members. I also discussed the questions involved with various civilians. One thing came out clearly. Most of the English witnesses believed that Indians could not be admitted to the highest and most responsible posts without serious detriment to the efficiency of the service. They believed that, as a general rule, Indians have not the nerve and judgment necessary in a critical situation. They believed, also, that Indians cannot be trusted to be impartial. For the majority of those who would hold office would be, as they now are, Brahmins; and Brahmins will favour Brahmins at the expense of other castes. They believed, therefore, that the transfer of the highest administrative posts to Indians would be very unpopular with the great mass of the people, for whom they genuinely believe themselves to be trustees. I am not in a position to estimate the truth of this view; but I believe it to be widely held among the English officials, and among the most intelligent and enlightened of them. On the other hand, the bulk of the Indian witnesses maintained that Indians trained in English ideas and methods would be as competent and fair as Englishmen. I must add, however, that I have met Indian officials who take the other view, and who hold that the time is not ripe for filling the highest posts with Indians.

The question of loyalty is even more difficult than that of efficiency, as, from an English point of view, it is more serious. There can, I think, be no doubt that very strong currents of disaffection are running among the educated class in India. This, it will be remembered, found violent expression a few years ago, at the time of the partition of Bengal. It has been driven underground since; but I believe that it is still strong, and that the causes which produce it are deep-seated and permanent. The first and chief of these is the growth of an Indian self-consciousness, a feeling of nationality, which itself is due to the British occupation. In English, Indians have for the first time a common language spoken by all educated people. Also, very largely under the stimulus of English and European scholars, they have recovered the heritage of their own philosophic and religious traditions; and they are reacting violently against the modes of thought which dominated an early generation. This movement—" back to the Vedas " one might call it—is not primarily political. But it almost inevitably takes a political cast. For it implies a reaction against all the ideas and ideals of the western world, the representatives of which in India are the English. The Arya Somaj, for instance, is primarily a society for educating Indians in their own religion, and for reforming by Indians, on Indian lines, what seems to be defective in their civilisation. But the association is generally regarded by the English as seditious; and I should think it quite probable that it really is so, indirectly if not directly; just as the Celtic movement in Ireland, though not political in its aim, carries with it political antagonism to the English, as a necessary adjunct to its æsthetic and religious antagonism. In short, in so far as Indians develop a self-consciousness which is fundamentally Indian in character, they must necessarily object more and more to control by a western race.

This antagonism of mental attitude is intensified and exasperated by the social gulf to which I have referred. Large numbers of Indians are educated in English universities. They find that in England an impalpable barrier separates them from their fellow-students; a barrier which is not deliberately created on either side, but results from different instincts, habits, and desires. Briefly, Indians seldom play games! On the other hand, socially they are treated in England as equals, and there is little consciousness on either side of a colour bar as such. They are isolated, but not irritated. When, however, they return to India, well instructed in democratic conceptions, social and political, they find a great difference; a difference which, one is told, manifests itself on the boat as soon as Suez is passed. The English in England do not feel that they are a governing race, and Indians a governed. They may be indifferent to Indians, they may be bored by them, but they have no sense of a superiority to be maintained. It is otherwise in India. There the English are a small camp of conquerors planted down among millions of conquered. Nothing can alter this fundamental fact. It is expressed everywhere and in everything. Unfortunately, it is sometimes expressed in frank and brutal insolence on the part of individual Englishmen. And Indians, being immensely sensitive, suspect insolence even where none is intended. Further, they have no adequate outlet for their ambition.

In the Civil Service they cannot rise to the highest posts; the Bar is overcrowded; they have little aptitude and no training for business; and they visit on the English their discontent at conditions for which the English are hardly directly responsible. Add that they are torn between two civilisations, out of touch with their own and excluded from ours. Indian society bores them, English society is not open to them; and in India it would only bore them if it were; for the English in India are of all the English the least intellectual and the least interested in ideas. Indians educated in England form, therefore, a natural centre for all seditious movements. The good and the bad elements of their character and their position alike make for this; their Indian patriotism, their personal vanity, their thwarted ambition, their idealism. They are, I think, of all gifted men—and they are often very gifted—the most unhappy. And their unhappiness makes them bitter and unjust.

In speaking thus far of the contact between East and West in India I have confined myself to what is peculiar to India, owing to the fact that it has been conquered, and is administered, by a western race. But apart from this fact, and the peculiar problems it creates, there is the larger and, from the point of view of general history, more important question of the general reaction between the civilisation of the East and that of the West. On this point, too, I must say a few words. Indian culture, I have suggested, is more remote from western than that of any other eastern country. And in India, as in China, the great masses of the people are, of course, untouched in their traditional ideas and way of life by any contact with the West. The effects, so far, of the British conquest on the peasants of India are economic rather than intellectual or spiritual; and on the economic question I do not propose to touch. On the other hand, the educated classes in India have been subjected for several generations to the full stream of western ideas; and its effects have been radical and profound. Born into a system of caste, they have been educated in the ideas of equal opportunity and no privilege. Born into an atmosphere of all-pervading religion, they have been educated in rationalism and free thought. Born into an atmosphere of faith, they have been educated in an atmosphere of science. The earlier generations accepted the new gospel whole-heartedly, repudiated with contempt the ideas, the customs, and (as was complained) the morals of their race; cut themselves off, in a word, from the whole Indian tradition. Then came a reaction against the West; and western-educated Indians now, I think, are generally sceptical both of the civilisation of the East and of that of the West. They may, indeed, sometimes defend their own fundamental institutions, such as caste and the position of women; they may praise the religious attitude of India; but I doubt whether this is often more than a kind of irritation against the shams of western civilisation, of which they are very fully conscious. The truth is that their experience of the West has opened the eyes of educated Indians to the weaknesses of their own system, though without converting them to the system of the West. And I cannot but believe that the process of disintegration must and will proceed to the end.

To speak first of what is most important, the general attitude towards life, the problem in India is essentially the same as it is everywhere in the modern world. How, if at all, can religion be reconciled with positive knowledge? The problem, indeed, is acuter in India than anywhere else, for India is more religious than any other country. On the other hand, it might be easier of solution than in western countries, for Indian religion has never been a system of dogmas, and is not entangled in questionable history. In India, it seems to me, you get the problem in its purest form, namely, not "did such-and-such events happen?" which is a purely historical question; nor "does the individual soul survive death?" which is perhaps unascertainable; but "is there a method of discovering truth about the world as a whole, and man's relation to it, other than the method of observation and induction?" Indian philosophy and religion have always affirmed that there is; that by meditation and discipline an internal perception is opened which is a perception of truth. Philosophically and *a priori* this position can neither be affirmed nor denied. It is entirely a matter of experience. Indians affirm that the experience occurs, and I have no doubt they affirm truly. They affirm also that it is not a hallucination or a merely subjective state, which may be questioned but cannot be refuted. To this fundamental point everything else is subordinate. The persistence of Indian religion will not depend on how much, or whether anything, in the Vedas is taken as gospel; it will depend on the continuous appearance and acceptance of the "saint" in the Indian sense of that term—the man, that is, who perceives what he affirms to be spiritual truth. Hitherto the line of the saints has not been cut off. One of the most remarkable of them, Sri Ramakrishna, died late in the nineteenth century; and any one who reads his conversations [1] will realise how little he depended on oral or written tradition, and how much on direct personal experience.

On the other hand, I cannot doubt that a training in positive science and its methods must make men more incapable either of having or desiring to have this experience, or of accepting it as evidential in others. Religion in some sense may be compatible with science; but only, I think, if religion be interpreted as a passionate contemplation of the world as made known by science, a sense of its complexity, its grandeur, and its immense,

[1] Gospel of Sri Ramakrishna, Madras, published by the Ramakrishna Mission, 1912.

overwhelming transcendence of man. This attitude may have analogies to that of Indian religion, but it is so far radically distinct that no Indian saint, and for that matter no Western saint, ever had anything but contempt for the knowledge gained by the senses and the intellect. Sainthood, in a word, is antagonistic to science, as science is antagonistic to sainthood. And the development in India of scientific knowledge and method must end by interrupting and destroying the old Indian religion in so far as that rests on a claim to attain truth by meditation divorced from observation.

There is then, I believe, in India as in Europe, a real, not merely seeming, antagonism between traditional religion and modern ways of thinking. The educated class is aware of this, and is making efforts analogous to those made in Europe to overcome it. These may take the form of an abstraction from all religions of their more rational elements and an emphasis of these as the essence of religion. This is the position of the Brahmo Somaj, which, in fact, is a pure theism, emphasising, however, the personal relation of the soul to God. To this sect, or rather these sects, for the society is split into several, all religions equally contain the truth, though all are tainted with error, and they make no special claim for the Hindu tradition or the Hindu sacred books. I should say, indeed, from what I saw, that their spirit is much more Christian than Hindu, though they do not give to Christ a higher position than to other great prophets. But for the very reason, perhaps, of its detachment from Hindu tradition, the Brahmo Somaj seems to be losing, not gaining, ground. It has few adherents outside Bengal, and my impression is that it exercises a small and declining influence. The Arya Somaj, on the other hand, bases itself on the Vedas, and is intensely national. It claims that its reformed faith is really the original faith of the Vedas, a claim which I should suppose would not for a moment be sustained by an impartial scholar. Its adherents have been very numerous and very active, especially in North-West India, and it has a college at Hardwar somewhat similar to Jesuit institutions, where boys are trained exclusively till they reach manhood in the tenets and spirit of the society, with a view to a future apostolate. The first generation of these students is now being sent out, and it will be interesting to learn what effect they will have on the world and the world on them. I got the impression, however, that the Arya Somaj, too, is declining with the disappearance of the first generation of its apostles. And, indeed, the attempt to graft a belief which shall be in harmony with modern ideas and modern social movements on the text of the Vedas is, I believe, as much foredoomed to failure as similar attempts in Europe to reconcile modern positive knowledge with the Old and the New Testament. Whatever may be the future of these particular sects, they are symptomatic of a crisis of thought which is world-wide, and arises wherever the spirit of modern science comes into contact with that of traditional religion. Meantime, however, the great mass of the Indian people, being uneducated even in reading and writing, continue unchanged in their old religious routine and religious sentiments. So that it is still true, as I suggested on an earlier page, that India is the most religious country in the world, unless Russia may be put on a level with her.

Turning now from religion to social institutions, there can be little doubt, I think, that caste, the most peculiar feature of Indian life, is being gradually undermined, partly by education, still more, perhaps, by railways and the gradual spread of industrialism. An example may show what I mean better than a page of generalisations. I was travelling in South India with a Brahmin in the carriage. What was he to do? He had to eat, and there was the carriage full of unclean foreigners. What he did do was to go into a corner of the carriage, get his servant to stand behind him, so as to make a kind of screen, and there on the floor dispose of the carefully prepared food he had brought with him in tin boxes. But this kind of thing must surely end in making the whole system look ridiculous. The best way to get rid of caste is to mix people up, and there is no such mixing as that of railway travel. Again, the introduction of factories must react upon caste, for caste is not taken account of by employers. At a mill which I visited in Agra I was told that the only difficulty caused by caste was in connection with Brahmins and with sweepers. No one would work with a sweeper, and a Brahmin may make trouble with any other caste. Otherwise, for industrial purposes, caste disappears. Caste, in short, will vanish as the social conditions which fostered it vanish; and these, I think, are bound to vanish whether or no the British rule is perpetuated, by the economic forces which now have the whole world in their grip.

The position of women, too, another peculiar feature of Indian civilisation, is being profoundly affected by Western influences. First, by the education of men, for educated men want educated wives. Secondly, by the education of girls, which is an important and growing feature of Indian life. Educated girls in India, as in other countries, marry later and demand more. In the present transition stage very real domestic tragedies result from the conflict between mothers-in-law brought up on the old system and daughters-in-law brought up on the new one, and this, perhaps, will happen for many generations. Still, for good or for evil, whoever rules India, and even if she rules herself, this change, I believe, will proceed. There is something in it world-wide and secular, and it is one of the profoundest social changes which the modern world is witnessing.

There is one other point on which I will touch, one to which I attach great importance, the effect of contact with the West on Indian arts and crafts. There can be no doubt that these generally have declined, if not perished; and the immediate cause is the competition of Western wares. This is most evident in textiles, where factory-made goods, mainly imported, but partly also manufactured in India, are killing the old domestic industries. But the decline seems to be general; I, at any rate, saw nowhere any modern products, whether in brasswork, wood-carving, embroidery, or enamel, which seemed to me to have any merit. To attribute this decline, however, merely to the competition of Western wares is not to go to the bottom of the matter. For the question remains, Why are Western wares preferred? The answer that they are cheaper is sufficient, no doubt, in the case of goods used by the mass of the people; cheapness, if you are poor, will override, in the East as in the West, all other considerations. But there is something more than this. Some Indian arts, that of painting, for instance, that of architecture on a grand scale, and the arts allied to it, always depended in India on the patronage of princes. These princes still exist and are still wealthy. But they prefer to patronise bad Western art. Why? Obviously because they have no real taste, and the prestige of the West overrides everything else in their mind. They want to have houses and clothes as like as possible to those of Europeans. And this raises the general question, to me a very interesting one, whether taste in all Oriental countries has not been for generations merely a habit; whether people went on making and using beautiful things merely because their fathers and grandfathers had done so; and as soon as anything new is offered, run to that, not only for the sake of cheapness, but for the sake of novelty and snobbery. My observations in China and in Japan, as well as in India, suggested to me very forcibly that this is the truth—that the arts of the East have long been dead, long before contact with the West, so far as active and intelligent taste is concerned, and that their collapse before the Western invasion is due not only to the cheapness of Western goods, but to an actual preference for them on other grounds, or, at any rate, an absence of preference for the more beautiful native products. Indians attribute the decline of their arts and crafts, as they attribute everything else, to the malign activities of the British Government. I believe they do not go deep enough. They should attribute it to the lack of effective and positive taste among their own leaders.

To sum up, I find in India a peculiar civilisation, antithetical to that of the West. I find a religious consciousness which negates what is really the religious postulate of the West, that life in time is the real and important life; and a social institution, caste, which negates the implicit assumption of the West, that the desirable thing is equality of opportunity. I find also that in India the contact between East and West assumes a form peculiarly acute and irritating, owing to the fact that India has been conquered and is governed by a Western Power. But the contact, none the less, is having the same disintegrating effect it produces in other Eastern countries. And I do not doubt that sooner or later, whether or no British rule maintains itself, the religious consciousness of India will be transformed by the methods and results of positive science, and its institutions by the economic influences of industrialism. In this transformation something, of course, will be lost. But my own opinion is that India has more to gain and less to lose by contact with the West than any other Eastern country.

PART II.—CHINA

WHEN I landed in China, indeed, when I first saw the Mongolian type at Darjeeling, I was aware of a feeling as though an oppressive cloud had lifted. I realised then how strange and how tragic India had been to me, how utterly alien I had felt there. The brooding over the whole country of a spirit not merely religious, but religious in a sense so remote from anything religion has meant in the West; the tremendous forces antagonistic to man marching over the land, famine, plague, malaria, drought, flood; the handful of English camped there, fighting these things with so little help and so little hope; the gulf between rulers and ruled; the spirit of revolt, which yet seemed to have in it no real capacity or promise; all these things, felt sub-consciously even more than consciously, had lain like a nightmare upon me, clouding all the interest and all the pleasure of my travels. India was sublime, but it was terrible. China, on the other hand, was human. At the first sight of these ugly, cheery, vigorous people I loved them. Their gaiety, as of children, their friendliness, their profound humanity, struck me from the first and remained with me to the last. I can imagine no greater contrast than that between their character, their institutions, their habits, and those of the Indians. The Chinese are, and always have been, profoundly secular, as the Indians are, and always have been, profoundly religious. It is true, of course, that the Chinese have had religion, as the Europeans have had it; Buddhism came to them from India as Christianity came to us from Judaea, and Taoism was an indigenous growth. They have had also saints and mystics, as Europe has had them. But Buddhism and Taoism have never suited the Chinese character any more than Christianity has suited the European. Both Buddhism and Taoism quickly degenerated to mere superstition, systems of magic, imaginary means to obtain material ends. It was, and is, Confucianism with its rationalism, its scepticism, its stress on conduct, that expresses the Chinese spirit. Over India gleam the stars; over China the sun shines. Mankind is the centre of the Chinese universe, as the Absolute is the centre of the Indian. Confucianism may easily be translated into terms of Western positivism; it could never be translated into terms of Hinduism. The religion of the mass of the Chinese has always been mere superstition, whereas in India, as I have said, it appears to be true that the superstition symbolises a real spiritualism. Ancestor worship is the centre of the Chinese system; but that, perhaps, ought not to be called worship at all. It is rather commemoration, and as such all educated Chinamen regard it.[1] It is thus rather a social than a religious institution, and serves to bind the family together rather than to foster a spiritual life. Its bearing on life is a bearing on conduct, and it is but an intensified form of the feeling which, even in the West, leads a man of distinguished family to feel that he must try to be worthy of his ancestors. What distinguishes the Chinese attitude in this matter from that of the modern West is its backward rather than its forward look.

[1] Probably only the educated. To the mass, I expect, it is really " worship," in the sense that they expect to receive benefits from the spirits to whom they offer.

We look to our descendants, they to their forebears. And the discrediting of Confucianism under the new *régime* is due to its supposed conservatism rather than to any idea that it is irrational and superstitious. In this matter of religion the Chinese have only to throw over their superstition—and over the educated superstition never had any hold—and they will be immediately in line with the West. In India, as we saw, things are far otherwise. For what is most characteristic and profound in the Indian spirit is antagonistic to and irreconcilable with rationalism and science.

This, which I call the secularism of the Chinese attitude to life, is also expressed in their art. The art of India, in my judgment, has, as art, little or no value (this, of course, is a highly controversial opinion), but it is tremendously significant of the spiritual life of India. It is all symbolic, and it is symbolic of those grandiose abstractions in which the Indian mind delights. It expresses an over-world of spiritual forces of which the world of sense is a shadowy and illusory manifestation. It does not interpret, it negates the ordinary life and the ordinary consciousness. That is why it is so disquieting, so terrible, so monstrous to the western spirit. But the art of China is through and through human. It is the kind of art that Romans, too, or Englishmen might have produced, if they had been gifted with æsthetic genius; the art of reasonable concrete-minded men, with a keen sensitiveness to the pathos and gaiety of human life, and the beauty and grandeur of nature. It is characteristic of Chinese landscape-painting that it should include representation of the human observer. Their artists do not, it is true, treat nature as a mere background to human life, as, for example, the great Venetian artists do; but neither do they treat it as the vehicle of tremendous supernatural forces, which is the spirit of Indian art. They treat it as a beautiful object, itself real, contemplated by a sane and sensitive human spirit. So with their poetry. It is of all poetry I know the most human and the least symbolic or romantic. It contemplates life just as it presents itself, without any veil of ideas, any rhetoric or sentiment; it simply clears away the obstruction which habit has built up between us and the beauty of things, and leaves that, showing in its own nature, revealed but not recreated.

Chinese art and Chinese poetry have the spirit of Wordsworth and of the most modern literary movement in France. Their art is a realism, though not an actualism; a vision of what this life is as seen by those who can see it, not of some other world behind or above or outside it.

The fundamental attitude of the Chinese towards life is thus, in my judgment, and always has been, that of the most modern West, nearer to us now than to our mediæval ancestors, infinitely nearer to us than India. And the same is true, at bottom, of social institutions. China, so far as I know, is the only country whose civilisation has been for centuries, if not always, democratic. There has never been caste in China, there has been, I think, less even of class than in most countries. That equality of opportunity which is the essence of democracy, and which has been denied by every other civilisation, has been affirmed by China in theory, and to a great extent in practice, from the date at which her written annals begin. There has never been a priestly caste, there has never been a governing caste. The rich, of course, have necessarily had advantages in the race as they have with us, but the barrier between rich and poor has never been as great as it is in the modern West, and it has been at least as easy, probably easier, to rise from bottom to top. And this social fact is reflected in the bearing and manners of the Chinese. I have never been in a country where the common people are at once so self-respecting, so independent, and so courteous. In America, for example, everybody appears to think it necessary to assure you that they are as good as you are by behaving rudely to you. Nothing of the kind obtains in China, for it would never occur to them that they are not as good. There is none of this self-conscious assertion of their rights; still less is there anything of that obsequiousness which one meets everywhere in India. The Chinese man is the democratic man. He is already, so far as his attitude to himself and to his fellows is concerned, what democrats hope the western man may become. His attitude is democratic, just as it is positive and secular. And this underlying and fundamental likeness to the man of the modern West is, in my judgment, far more important and significant than the superficial differences which are usually dwelt upon by western travellers and residents.

There is one other important point in which China contrasts with India. China has been and remains politically independent and united. This statement needs some qualification, but it is essentially true. The Tartars and the Manchus have conquered China, but they have imposed on her nothing but a dynasty. They have adopted completely the manners, customs, ideas of the conquered. Of China it is truer even than of Greece that *Capta ferum victorem cepit.* Not so India. The Mahometans, in spite of conversions, remain Mahometans, different in religion, different in sentiment, different in social institutions, from the Hindus. Nothing yet has brought the two communities into harmony; and their antagonism is still, and perhaps increasingly, an important factor in the Indian situation. Again, India, until the British conquest, has never been welded into a political unity. The largest native empires, like that of Asoka, the largest alien ones, like that of the Moguls, never included the whole peninsula. And, in addition, there have been always the vertical divisions of caste.

But China, except for short periods, has been for two thousand years at least under one head; and though the provinces have had a very large measure of autonomy, they have been administered by officials appointed by the Central Government, and have recognised its existence by the payment of taxes. The various dialects of China, though unintelligible one to another, are varieties of the same language; and the common script has always given to the educated a common medium of communication, much as Latin gave it to mediæval Europe. China has been a political unity, even though a loose one; and though this unity has not given rise to a strong national feeling, there is in China a basis for such feeling more real and more powerful than anything that seems to exist in India. For this reason, among others, China would not be so easy to conquer as India was, nor so easy to govern by any race that did not assimilate itself to Chinese customs and standards.

I see, then, in China, so far as the most fundamental conditions are concerned, a far greater similarity to the modern West than to India. But, of course, points of similarity to India and of difference from the West do strike the eye. Like India, but unlike western Europe, China is predominantly agricultural, and the bulk of her people are peasants. Like India, and unlike the West, indeed to a much greater degree than India, she is untouched by industrialism. The era of railways, of mines, of factories, is but just beginning, and the immense resources of the country have hardly been tapped. Like India, and unlike the modern West, the family is the cardinal point on which all her social life and a great part of her government turns. And this family solidarity, while it fulfils many of the functions which in the West have to be undertaken by Government, is a very serious obstacle to the introduction of western forms of business—for example, the joint-stock company. Still, these differences, important as they are, are comparatively superficial; and it would, I believe, for good or for evil, be much easier to westernise China than it would be to westernise India. The Chinese would only have to apply their attitude to life in a new way; but the Indians would have to transform theirs. The Chinese are already secular, practical, matter-of-fact; they require, to westernise them, only a new technique. But the Indians require a new spirit.

Although, however, as I have suggested, it would be easier to westernise China than to westernise India, the process of westernisation has not as yet gone so far in the one country as in the other. Effective contact between Europe and China dates only from the opium war.[1] From that date the activities of the western powers in China have been continuous, discreditable, and indefensible. But though the powers have robbed China, have bullied her, have interfered with her independence and sovereign rights, have imposed upon her teaching which she did not want and trade which she thought disastrous and immoral, they have so far made no serious attempt to conquer and annex her. The servitude of China is financial; but the history of Egypt shows how easily financial may pass into political control. It may be so with China; the next few months or years will decide. But meantime and up to now China is independent. The activities, commercial and other, of the foreigners have been

[1] In spite of Mr. Morse's apologies, I consider this to be the proper description of that war.

mostly confined to the treaty ports. And though these are now very numerous and include a number of cities far inland on the Yang-tze, they are of course but isolated points in the vast territory of China. And even in these ports the western spirit has hardly touched even the externals of Chinese life. The foreign communities build their own cities outside the native city; there they administer themselves, lead their own life as in Europe, their life of business and of sport, and never, if they can help it, enter the native city or any part of the interior of China. The British firms, who were first in the field, did and still do their business through the medium of Chinese merchants, and have no direct relation with their customers in the country. They never stir from the treaty ports, and they know nothing and care nothing about Chinese conditions except so far as these may react upon their business. "We see too much of things Chinese here," the agent of a British firm said to me, when I made some comment on the Chinese city. And the sentiment, I believe, is pretty general among Europeans in China.

While these conditions prevailed there was nothing in the presence of the foreign traders which need have led to any radical change in Chinese institutions or ideas. But the conditions are now rapidly changing. The new enterprise, especially of Germans and Japanese, is sending bagmen acquainted with the language all over the interior of China. Oil and cigarettes are the pioneers of this commercial invasion. The skin-disease of advertisement is beginning to disfigure the face of the country, and German *art nouveau* appears in the stations of the railway from Tsinan-fu to Pekin. The grip of the West has begun to close, and will more and more be felt in the general dissemination of ugliness, meanness, and insincerity throughout the empire.

More important, however, I think, than commercial enterprise in disturbing the secular tradition of China has been missionary activity. I did not, indeed, gather, and I do not believe, that China is in process of Christianisation or will ever be Christianised, though I have met Chinese Christians and, I think, sincere ones. But the missionaries have been the pioneers of western education, and it is western education that has made the revolution. All the new leaders have been educated, first at missionary schools and colleges in China, then abroad, mainly in Japan and the United States. And this education has produced a new and surprising type of Chinese. Nothing in my travels has struck and perplexed me more than this. China has always been regarded as the type of the unchanging. If ever there was a stable national character, a stable national mentality, it might have been supposed that it would be there, in a homogeneous people of the same stock, never conquered, or at least never affected in race, in manners, in laws, in language, by conquest; never interrupted or disturbed for centuries in their traditional ideas and their traditional manner of life. Here, surely, if anywhere, sudden revolution was impossible. Here change, if it came at all, would come by slow degrees, fighting its way against an immense and profound psychological immobility. But what happens in fact? A Chinese taken as a boy and brought up in a missionary school, then transferred during the impressionable period of life to a foreign country to complete his education, returns to China transformed through and through. There is no vestige of conservatism left in him. He has adopted not only the manners, the dress, the speech, the very intonation of a foreign country; he has adopted its whole mental and moral outfit. There is nothing in China he does not want to transform, nothing he does not believe he can transform. This is particularly true of the Chinese educated in America. I met in Canton some of the chief officials of the revolutionary government, the chief justice, the foreign secretary and others. I was astounded. They were exactly like American undergraduates. Their whole mentality, so far as I could see, was American. They had not only the manners, the dress, the speech; they had the confidence, the light-heartedness, the easy and disconcerting superficiality. On the other hand, those educated in England were comparatively critical, sober, and cautious. Those educated in Japan, I was informed, had the revolutionary *élan* of that country; and when the second revolution broke out, the students that were in Japan crowded over *en masse* to join the revolutionary troops. The one student I met from Germany looked and spoke like a German. This conversion may, of course, be superficial. There may be underlying it an unchanged basis of Chinese character. But if so, it is the superficial part that is active in China. It is these young men that have made the revolution and established the Republic; that are doing all they can to sweep away the old China, root and branch, and build up there a reproduction of America. There is nothing, I think, which they would not alter if they could, from the streets of Canton to the family system, from the costume of a policeman to the national religion. This attitude of theirs exasperates the foreigners, who seem as much disgusted and alarmed at the actual appearance of a new China as they used to be critical and censorious of the old one. But it is, after all, very natural. These young men find their country a prey to foreign aggression. They see that the only way to meet the foreigners is to meet them on their own ground, and they have before them the triumphantly successful example of Japan. It must, however, be admitted that there has not appeared in China any group of men of the capacity and power of the statesmen who piloted Japan into the new era. The young men have ideas in plenty, but they have no experience, and, it would seem, no practical capacity. Too often they have not character. For it is, I fear, indisputable, as it is undisputed, that many of the new officials and of the new legislators are corrupt as well as incompetent. Certainly it is remarkable and, so far as my knowledge of history goes, unique that in a great revolution in a nation of four hundred millions one man only should emerge with the capacity for government; and Yuan Shih Kai, I believe, will not appear to history to be more than an astute and tenacious opportunist. The recent revolution has exposed the incapacity and the lack of character of the southern leaders. And, however sympathetic one may be with the revolutionists, the question forces itself upon one whether we have not here another demonstration that old bottles will not hold new wine; that ideas derived from an alien civilisation may transform the brain, but cannot penetrate the soul of a different race. I suspect, at any rate, that in young China there is some dislocation between their convictions and their character, which makes them ineffective for action towards ends in which they genuinely believe.

On the other hand, the problem before the republican revolutionaries is a vast one, and one which no country has solved without years of confusion and bloodshed. European critics are apt to forget this. It took France a century of successive revolutions and reactions before the Republic was definitely established. Two revolutions and a series of civil wars were necessary to get rid of the Stuarts in England. The surprising thing in China is that the dynasty has disappeared with so little effort and so little regret. For among all the possibilities of the future, the one which is universally repudiated is a Manchu restoration. Still, to get rid of the Manchus is one thing, to set up a new government is another. The breach of continuity has been complete, as complete as in revolutionary France. Nothing in Chinese history or tradition has prepared them for a representative republic, and it is quite possible that it is not under a republic that the new era, which in any case is inevitable, will be best inaugurated and furthered. At present, however, it must be admitted that republican institutions have not been given a fair chance. That, I believe, has been the weakness of the President's policy. Instead of endeavouring to gain the confidence of all parties in the National Assembly, and to get all to work together for the common good, he seems to have set out from the beginning to discredit the Assembly. When I was in Pekin the two Houses were meeting day after day and doing no business because a quorum could not be obtained; and this was due to the deliberate abstension of the Chin-Pu-Tang party, which is admittedly the party of the President, and which, no doubt, was in his pay. True, serious differences of policy had developed between him and the southern party. He had contracted the quintuple loan over the head of the Assembly in defiance of their protest and in violation of the spirit, if not the letter, of the constitution. But the fact that he did so is precisely an example of what I should call his bad statesmanship. What is worse, he was believed to be privy to the assassination of Sung, the southern leader; and as the facts have never been allowed to come out in Court, he must continue to lie under that suspicion. If the National Assembly hitherto has been impotent and futile, the fault, I believe, lies rather with the President than with them.[1] But these, after all, are

[1] Since this was written, the President has dissolved all elective bodies in China, and made himself an absolute dictator.

transitory conditions. The fundamental fact is that the revolution was accomplished by a handful of men educated in foreign customs and foreign ideas, and working with a mercenary army (for it is clear that the troops who have taken part on either side are mercenaries who transfer their allegiance from one party to the other according as they are paid). There is no national movement in China, for there is no Chinese nation, in the sense that there is an English or a French or a German nation. The Chinese, as I have already pointed out, though they have never been divided as India has, have never been united by a common political consciousness. Their social organisation has rested not on the central government, but on the family and the village. Government has been a mechanism imposed from above to make roads and canals, to do justice, and to collect taxes. And the comparative isolation of China for many centuries, the absence of wars waged for very existence, such as have built up the European system, prevented the formation of national sentiment by outside pressure. The Chinese have been the most peaceable, and, in many respects, the most civilised people the world has seen.

They have not had, because they have not needed, a national self-consciousness, and they cannot improvise one in a moment. There can be no doubt, I imagine, that the mass of the people do not know what the revolution is about; and that they welcomed it less because it got rid of the Manchus than because it relieved them for a time from the payment of taxes.

It does not, however, follow, as European critics often imply, that China can never acquire a political sense or work a constitution. Given education, a press, better means of communication, and in a generation the change might be effected. The Chinese, as experience has now shown, are the most educable of people; and this, no doubt, applies to the masses no less than to the handful who have hitherto had the opportunity. And the education has begun. In elementary schools modern subjects are beginning to be taught; geography, history, elementary science, the existence, the character, and the power of other nations. I myself, visiting a school in a small village on the Upper Yangtze, far from all foreign influence, found an English-speaking teacher who had been educated by missionaries, an English spelling and reading book, maps of China and of the world, and drawings of bacteria. These things must be taking effect. And those who seem still to think that the revolution in China is a mere flash in the pan, implying no radical transformation, are likely before many years have passed to be very much astonished. What may happen politically, whether the government be republican or monarchical, on the American or the French or the German model, is comparatively unimportant. The important thing is that the educational process has begun, the education both of events and of schooling; and that to education the Chinese are eminently responsive. For good and for evil the old China is a thing of the past. The penetration by western ideas has begun, and whether it go faster or slower it will go far and go to the end.

PART III.—JAPAN

TURNING now to Japan I find here, too, affinities with the West and contrasts with India. Japan is the only country I have visited which reminds me of what I suppose ancient Greece to have been. This, at any rate, is true of externals. The costume of the men, leaving bare the legs and arms, and their perfect proportions and development, were a constant delight to me. The most Hellenic thing I ever saw was a group of Japanese youths practising jiu-jitsu naked under the trees of a temple garden, or by moonlight on the seashore. Again, the Japanese theatre must be more like the theatre of ancient Greece than anything now extant. The audience in their loose white robes; the magnificent posing of the actors; the chant in which the text is declaimed; the dance; the choice, for subject, of ancient heroic legend, all these are striking points of resemblance. And though, as Mr. Archer has pointed out, the actual form of the theatre recalls rather Elizabethan than Greek conditions, the total effect to my judgment was much more Hellenic than Shakespearean. Again, in Japan, as in ancient Greece, there is a universal prevalence of art. The skill and the taste still persist. Every common thing is beautiful, the cups, the tea-pots, even the very toys. The houses, from the æsthetic point of view, are the most perfect ever designed. Fineness of taste and skill of hand seem to be general, save where the western invasion has destroyed them. Add to this the impression one receives in Japan of a people "simple, sensuous, and passionate," quick to laugh, quick to quarrel, quick to die, or kill, in everything intense and unreflective, and you get a resemblance with the Greeks which is, I think, more than superficial. The points in which the Japanese character and creation are unlike and inferior to the Greek depend upon their comparative lack of intellect. The Greeks were the originators in the West of philosophy and science, and their literature is as remarkable for its intellectual content as for its æsthetic form. The Japanese have originated nothing; they took all their ideas from China; and their literature and art is curiously unintellectual. Their whole civilisation, indeed, beautiful and passionate as it is, is thin and simple when compared with that of ancient Greece. If, in a word, Japan is the Greece of the East, it is a Greece without Socrates, Plato, Aristotle, Sophocles, Thucydides. A curiously truncated Greece! Yet, I think, the foundation, so to speak, is the same. The same temperament, passionate and æsthetic; only a lack of the critical and constructive power of mind which has made the Greeks, after the lapse of two thousand years, still the living masters of the West.

But it is, of course, not only with ancient Greece that the civilisation of Japan presents important analogies. In institutions, and in all those aspects of character which are affected by institutions, it was, until the revolution, an almost complete reproduction of mediæval Europe. Japanese feudalism was, in every point, similar to European, save that it was simpler and intenser, and, of course, uncomplicated by the influences, ethical, social, and political, of the Catholic Church. If the essentials of feudalism be, as I think they are, a hierarchic organisation of society under the rule of a military caste, and the predominance, in the scheme of virtues, of those peculiar to that caste—courage, loyalty to a chief, and personal honour—then Japanese feudalism, which lasted up to the revolution of the nineteenth century, presents an exact parallel to feudalism in Europe. And its virtues and qualities still persist in Japan; they are said to have been, and no doubt were, the secret of their success in the war with Russia; and they constitute the greatest distinction between Japanese civilisation and that of India or of China on the one hand, and of the West on the other. It is for that reason that I say chivalry is the dominant note of Japanese civilisation, understanding by chivalry the qualities fostered by a feudal *régime*. These qualities are summed up in the Japanese term "bushido," and they centre about the national religion of Shintoism, the essence of which is devotion to ancestors, and in particular to the divine ancestors of the Emperor. Shintoism is the true religion of Japan; and it was a sound instinct (though, as it turned out, the policy prompted by it was a failure) which led the statesmen of the new era to foster Shintoism at the expense of Buddhism. For

Buddhism, though it has had great influence in Japan, as is testified by the innumerable temples which are the chief beauty of the country, and the tender and profound religious art of the earlier period, was really as alien to the Japanese spirit as Christianity to the European. The Japanese are not by nature, any more than the Chinese, disbelievers in life. They are active, sensuous, ambitious, at need aggressive. They have to an eminent degree the qualities of citizens and patriots; and the influence of Buddhism has been with them more æsthetic than ethical. Japanese feudalism converted the Buddha's doctrine of renunciation into the Stoicism of the warrior. The Japanese Samurai renounced desire, not that he might enter Nirvana, but that he might acquire the contempt of life which would make him a perfect warrior. In him, the knight included and swallowed up the saint. And the Samurai, meditating in a teahouse on the beauty, the brevity, and the pathos of life, and passing out to kill or to die, is as typical of the Japanese attitude to life as the wandering Sannyasin is of the Indian.

But this civilisation of Japan, so complete, so simple, so homogeneous—a military system preserved, oddly enough, without degeneration, through more than two centuries of peace, and deliberately secluded from all influences from without that might have disturbed it—is already a thing of the past. As in India, as in China, as all over the world, the aggressive western powers forced themselves and their ideals upon the reluctant nation. But Japan, a small homogeneous, military State, inspired by a strong patriotic sentiment, met the advance in quite a different way from any other nation. In order to avoid being westernised by the powers she decided to westernise herself. To save her life she made up her mind to lose it. The system she had cherished so carefully she threw overboard almost in a day; and a generation saw a centralised monarchy substituted for a nominal suzerainty, the military caste converted into officers in a national army, education in science, theoretical and applied, substituted for education in the Chinese and Japanese classics, feudalism abolished, and industrialism triumphantly inaugurated. I know of nothing in history analogous to this extraordinary transformation except the earlier conversion of Japan to Chinese ideals and practice. I proceed to comment more in detail on some aspects of this transformation.

To take first externals. In Japan, as in India and in China, but in Japan in pre-eminent degree, one is struck by the rout of æsthetic taste before the western invasion. In old Japan, roughly, everything was beautiful; in modern Japan everything is hideous. Fortunately, in externals, old Japan is almost everywhere in evidence. It is in a few great cities that the change appears. Tokyo, for example, is becoming ugly with an intensity of ugliness I have seen nowhere else. The modern buildings in European style are as meaningless and as dead as all architecture in the West, and they have not the compensation of that kind of Egyptian slave-made impressiveness which characterises recent building in western capitals. The statues in the European style have a grotesque monstrosity which makes even the monuments of London appear dignified by comparison. The European costume of the official and educated classes—fortunately the mass of the people still adhere to the Japanese style—is a model of vulgarity and ineptitude. Japanese taste is altogether disoriented as soon as it has to deal with European and American conventions. Perhaps, as I have already suggested, the taste had really long ceased to exist, and become a mere habit with no power of resistance. However that may be, it is fortunate that so far, in most crafts, the old tradition still persists, and Japanese pottery, lacquer, weaving, and embroidery are still being produced not unworthy of their artistic past. How long this may continue I cannot prophesy. A general extension of the factory system would of course destroy it. Some Japanese, it is true, are aware of the value of their own traditions and of the devastating effect of industrialism on art and beauty, and may possibly make a successful effort to conserve what they still possess. I confess, however, that I am not very hopeful of this. For among educated Japanese I have met few who seem to care about such things, and these few were apt to be conservative and reactionary, and without much practical influence. The terrible prestige of the West covers and recommends everything bad in it as well as everything good, and the Japanese, most imitative of nations, seem to desire only to be able to say at every point that they are as good as the most advanced western nation.

Turning from this, to my mind, very important point, to those social and political questions which in the present age almost monopolise public attention, the entry of Japan into the western industrial system is carrying with it all the consequences which that system has produced in Europe and America. There is a gradual exodus from the country to the town, due to what is now felt to be the dulness and the lack of opportunity of life on the soil, and the attraction of superior wages. Pauperism, unknown under the old *régime*, is becoming a problem, and though there is no poor law in Japan, there appears to be need for one. Unemployment is beginning to show itself; and the factory system is developing abuses similar to those which disgraced its early history in Europe, abuses which the Japanese have not yet begun to combat by legislation. For though there is a factory law on the Statute Book, it has not yet been put into operation, ostensibly on the ground of lack of funds, really, as I was informed, because of the influence with the Government of the great manufacturers. The growth of national wealth, in short, is being accompanied by all those evils of disorganisation and unjust distribution which constitute the political and social problem of the West. And these evils are intensified by a financial system which raises the bulk of the national revenue by taxes on the necessities of the poor.

This brings me to the question of the Government of Japan, a system which has been much praised, but which seemed to me, in its practical operation, to be the worst and most ominous factor in the present situation. Traditionally, as is well known, the political and national sentiment of Japan centred about the Emperor. The sentiment, no doubt, was obscured during the period of the Shogunate, when the Emperor was a mere figurehead. But long before the aggression of the West produced the great crisis an internal movement was working for the restoration of the Mikado's power. That restoration was effected by the revolution of 1867, and effected by the voluntary abdication of the Shogun. And the tradition of personal loyalty to the Emperor, as an actual descendant and representative of gods, the tradition, that is, in a very intense form, of his divine right, was an asset which the statesmen of the revolution were not likely to throw away in laying the foundations of modern Japan. When, therefore, they made a constitution they naturally turned for a model rather to Germany than to America or France or England. They made the Emperor the centre of the whole political structure, and clause after clause in the constitution endeavours to secure, so far as the letter of the law can do it, that monarchical government in Japan shall never be transformed into parliamentary government as we have it in England. To foster this feeling about the Emperor, the machinery of public education is brought to bear. On stated anniversaries the children do reverence to the Mikado's portrait. His proclamation, which makes himself and his divine ancestors the source and centre of all the history and polity of Japan, is the text on which all moral instruction is a commentary. A deliberate attempt is made to mould the mind of young Japan to religious veneration for the head of the State; and to this general attitude all domestic and personal morality is subordinated. The Emperor is put forward as the head, not only of the political, but of the social and ethical structure of Japan. It is, however, interesting to note that in spite of the position thus given to the Emperor, he does not, in fact, appear to govern in person. Until recently he governed through and by and, it would seem, in subordination to the remarkable group of men called the elder statesmen; a group as much unknown to the constitution as the Cabinet is in England, and owing their position to the confidence of the sovereign, and to their prestige and influence among the officers of the army and navy. It is these men hitherto that have governed Japan. Their ideal is bureaucratic. They have never desired or intended that the representative element in the constitution should become the governing element, or that public opinion should reach that stage of development in which it can really dictate to ministers. This policy they have pursued with the ruthless and intelligent pertinacity which appears to belong to the Japanese character. There is, in fact, in Japan, whatever the letter of the law may be, very little liberty in the matter of organising and directing public sentiment. Trade unions, though permitted by the law, are prevented by police regulation from directing their activity to the raising of wages or shortening of hours, by combination and the threat of a strike. I met a man who had been imprisoned for some months for encouraging men on strike, and whose whole activity, in a social settlement he had attempted to found, had been suppressed by the authorities. I heard of another who had been imprisoned for five years for making some comment not regarded as respectful on a public distribution of alms by the Emperor. In the face of this suppressive activity of the executive, the representative House seems to be powerless. Parties are still grouped about persons, not about principles, and the desire for office and the emoluments and advantages it may bring with it seems to emasculate leaders and followers alike. The very professors in the Imperial universities feel that they are muzzled on all subjects touching public affairs; for though, of course, they would not be ostensibly punished for their opinions, they know well that advancement depends on pleasing those in power. The hand of the bureaucracy lies heavy on Japan; and if it secures, as it seems to do in many departments, efficiency of administration, it secures it at the expense of liberty.

This system, however, of government by a clique of nobles, backed by the prestige of the Emperor and using the forms of the Constitution, is hardly likely to continue indefinitely. In the first place, the peculiar sanctity attached to the Emperor's person can hardly survive in a people that is daily becoming more and more penetrated by the western spirit of rationalism and criticism. The Japanese, even the Japanese masses, will not long be able to maintain the fiction that a man is a god. The very existence of a constitution is a contradiction to the principle of divine right, as much in Japan as once in France, and now in Germany. For a constitution implies, if it does not affirm, the opposite principle of the right of the people. And however much it may be formally provided that an elected assembly is only to be consultative, all history shows that it will end by making a bid for supremacy. So far as I could ascertain, the movement in this direction has already begun in Japan. The chief political leaders seem to have paid at least lip-service to the doctrine that a minister ought to command a majority in the representative House. The fall of Prince Katsura's ministry was brought about by the pressure of public opinion, aided by rioting in the capital; and it is noticeable that in that crisis, for the first time, the name of the Emperor was dragged into political controversy. The narrow basis of representation in Japan, which confines the electorate to the upper middle class, will no doubt delay a democratic evolution. But the modern history of France and of England shows that such barriers generally disappear once public opinion is effectively aroused. There are signs, I think, that it is stirring in Japan, and its manifestations are likely to be the more violent the more it is denied the normal outlet. In a word, the Japanese statesmen are endeavouring to combine an autocratic system of government with an industrial civilisation, a free press, and an education on western lines. This I believe to be as impossible in the long run as it is to keep water in the liquid state after the boiling point is reached. Government follows social evolution; and industrialism, though it may favour plutocracy, can never favour the domination of a military caste.

In this connection I may briefly observe that the educational system I have described, whereby loyalty to the Emperor is made the pivot of morality, seems to be producing on the youth of the country the opposite effect to that intended. They react violently, I was told, from this governmental pressure; they suspect, not without reason, the sincerity of their teachers, and emerge from the system with a bias rather sceptical or democratic than monarchical.

My impression, then, of modern Japan is briefly this: I find a people moulded by centuries of feudal institutions and feudal morality, homogeneous, patriotic, and with their natural self-reliance and pride intensified by the rapidity and ease with which they have assimilated the teaching of western civilisation, and raised to a white heat by their victory over Russia. At the same time I find that their very success is undermining the basis on which that success rests. The extension of industrialism means the substitution of industrial for feudal psychology and ethics, the disappearance of the old, simple cult of the Emperor, which made it a matter of course to die for him, and a dislocation of all social relations, which has as its immediate effect pauperism, unemployment, unrest, and discontent. Add to this a heavy burden of debt, incurred mainly by the Russian war, pressing on a country not rich in natural resources, and a population too numerous to be supported in comfort on their own territory; a governmental *régime* which discourages and suppresses popular association and popular agitation; and a financial system which throws the burden of taxation on the poor. The past and the present, oriental tradition and western culture, are at grips in Japan more intensely than in any other country; but in Japan alone the issue of the conflict will be determined by the people themselves, not by the pressure of foreign powers.

CONCLUSION

As a result of this survey of the present condition of the principal countries of the Far East, I find myself face to face with one of the fundamental issues of modern civilisation. The East, it is clear to me, has developed types of life having beauties and advantages which we have lost in the modern West. The great mass of the people live, as they always have lived, on the soil. They have a hard life, a life exposed to great physical disasters, a life at the mercy of nature. But also, it is a life *in* nature; and though the people may not be consciously alive to the beauties and sublimities of the natural world, I cannot doubt that they are aware of them and derive from them, if not happiness, at least a certain dignity and breadth of outlook. We ought not, on this point, to generalise from our own agricultural labourers, and infer a necessary degradation as the consequence of life on the soil. It is the peasants we have destroyed, those who lived on the land when England was

" merry England," in whom we ought to seek an analogy for the life of Oriental peasants; and these, I suspect, have a solidity, a sense of the fundamental realities, and the possibility of a really religious outlook on the world which it will be hard to parallel among city dwellers.

Again, throughout all the East there has been a development of culture in some respects more important and higher than that of the modern West. Under culture I include religion, literature, and art. And I regard these, not as being, in themselves, the purpose of human life, but rather as signs that that purpose is being fulfilled; that men, having satisfied, without too much exertion and exhaustion, their material needs, are living a life of rich and fine feeling, are contemplating nature and their own lives and purposes in rituals, pictures, poems, and songs. This kind of culture the East, I think, has always had in a finer sense than the modern West.

On the other hand, for causes which it would be interesting to try to trace, the East has fallen far behind the West in what I may call the machinery of life, and in all that kind of intellectual effort and achievement on which the command of that machinery depends. The West has invented, if not science, the applied sciences; and in so doing has made the externals of life, for the well-to-do at any rate, and perhaps also, when all is said, for the poor, immensely more comfortable than they have ever been before. It has made it possible for a much greater number of people to live on a given area; but at the same time it has almost destroyed the beauty of life and the faculty of disinterested contemplation. It is not really creditable, in the West, to be anything but a man of business, in the widest sense of the term; to live in any way which cannot be shown directly or indirectly to increase the comforts and facilities of life or diminish its detriments. This, of course, is especially true of the new countries, where there are no traditions and no ancient culture; but it is becoming increasingly true in Europe too. Now I do not myself think that this attitude is merely contemptible, and convicts the West of sheer materialism. I believe that, under all this, hardly conscious of itself, is a great impulse which may fairly be called spiritual. The West is doing more than it knows it is doing; it is endeavouring to lift the general level of material life in order that there may be more leisure, more education, more capacity and opportunity for that impassioned reflection on life which is the essence of what I mean by culture. The preoccupation of the West with material things does not really imply materialism; and it necessitates an intensity of life, a development of brain and will-power hitherto unknown in the history of the soul.

Still, the pace at which we are living, the competition of every kind, the intensity, the fatigue, the nerve-strain, involve a dislocation of the moral equilibrium of life. The East lives, and has always lived, at a lower tension; but it has kept a better balance between the active and the contemplative faculties. It is in that balance that I see civilisation. The West will have to recover it, and I used to think that it might learn to recover it from the East; that it might take from the East, and the East from it, what each required, and that a synthesis might result which would be more comprehensively human. My journey to the East has somewhat shaken my belief in this possibility. Civilisation is a whole. Its art, its religion, its way of life, all hang together with its economic and technical development. I doubt whether a nation can pick and choose; whether, for instance, the East can say, "We will take from the West its battle-ships, its factories, its medical science; we will not take its social confusion, its hurry and fatigue, its ugliness, its over-emphasis on activity." So, also, I doubt whether the West can say, "We will take from India its contemplative and religious spirit; but we will maintain our own pre-eminence in the material arts, our popular and democratic institutions, our science, theoretic and applied." The West may receive a stimulus from the East, it can hardly take an example; and the East, taking from the West its industrial organisation, will have to take everything else.

I should look, therefore, for a redress of the balance in the West, not directly to the importation of ideals from the East, but to a reaction prompted by its own sense of its excesses on the side of activity. And on the other hand, I expect the East to follow us, whether it like it or no, into all these excesses, and to go right through, not round, all that we have been through on its way to a higher phase of civilisation. In short, I believe that the renewal of art, of contemplation, of religion, will arise in the West of its own impulse; and that the East will lose what remains of its achievement in these directions and become as "materialistic" (to use the word) as the West, before it can recover a new and genuine spiritual life.

THE TEMPLE PRESS, PRINTERS, LETCHWORTH